SMILING DAVID

Other screenplays by Jeremy Sandford

Hotel de Luxe
ACTT best Television Documentary

Cathy Come Home
Writers Guild Best Television Play
Italia Prize

Edna, the Inebriate Woman
Writers Guild Best Television Play
Critics Choice Best Television Play

Other books by Jeremy Sandford

Cathy Come Home
Edna, the Inebriate Woman
Synthetic Fun
Down and Out in Britain
Gypsies
In Search of the Magic Mushroom
Tomorrow's People

SMILING DAVID

The Story of David Oluwale

By

Jeremy Sandford

*'What should a constable do
with these vagrants?'*

Leeds newspaper

CALDER & BOYARS
LONDON

First published in Great Britain 1974
by Calder & Boyars Ltd.
18 Brewer Street, London W1R 4AS

ALL RIGHTS RESERVED
ISBN 0 7145 1048 3 Casebound edition
ISBN 0 7145 1049 1 Paperback edition

Illustrations by courtesy of the *Yorkshire Post* and *The Sunday Times*.

Printed by Whitstable Litho, Millstrood Road, Whitstable, Kent.

CONTENTS

ILLUSTRATIONS

Pictures by courtesy of the Yorkshire Post and The Sunday Times.

PREFACE

David Oluwale died in the midst of a typical British town in the daylight of an early April morning.

Most of the social services knew, in the years leading to his death, that he was going down.

Most of the charities knew of David and the police and prison services knew about him.

Many were of the opinion that he could not live long.

Yet the entire panoply of the Welfare State seems to have been powerless to prevent his death.

David's slow destruction gives the lie to the claim that we have achieved the 'just society' in Britain.

I have invented nothing in this script—he is unique among the 'dosser' population in that there is already so much documentation in existence on the subject of David that it is not necessary to invent.

When scripting the part of David, I have used only those words which people can actually remember him speaking to them.

All details are accurate and the court scenes are verbatim, although I have changed or removed names where I thought that their inclusion might cause harm to individuals.

This script has been simplified to make it easier to read. I have omitted some of the instructions which establish the exact relationship between voice and vision.

Jeremy Sandford

Smiling David, then known as *Oluwale*, was first performed on BBC Radio Brighton as part of the Brighton Festival in May 1972.

Narrator: PAUL SCOFIELD
Other Voices:

EDWARD CHAPMAN	DESMOND NEWLING
PETER CLEAL	JAN NEWLING
DAVID COLLINGS	BOB OKENEDO
RITA DAVIES	PETER PACEY
MONA HAMMOND	RENU SETNA
RAM JOHN HOLDER	MADHAV SHARMA
ZARA JABER	PAMELA SLADE
HORACE HAMES	EDDIE TAGOE
LOCKWOOD WEST	

Technical direction was by CHRISTOPHER TANDY and the programme was produced in the studios of BBC Radio Brighton by KEITH SLADE.
The film rights for *Smiling David* were bought by Harlech Television in 1974.

The author wishes to thank Bromley Davenport of NACRO, who first suggested that he should undertake this work, and also acknowledge the help given by the many citizens of Leeds in his research.

SMILING DAVID

CAST

BLACKS
About ten Nigerians.
About ten West Indians.
A Sikh.
A Pakistani.
An Indian.
A Muslim.
Mr. Noel.
David Oluwale.

WHITES
About ten officials of various sorts.
Maureen, 35, friendly to blacks.
Mary, probation officer.
Mr. Cobb.
P.C. Seager.
White Idealist.
The Inspector.
The Sergeant.
The Constable.
The Inspector's Wife.
Gladys, David's Wife.
Mr. Bottomley.

LAGOS

Seascape

*A wide sweeping bay in the
vicinity of Lagos.
All the dogs are barking in
Lagos.*

Townscape

*Nigerian music.
Various shots show the lively
street life in Lagos. Music
continues.*

Mountain

*A boy sits up in the mountain.
He is DAVID (aged 6). Two or
three other BOYS.
It is the mid-1930s.*

Catholic Mission School

CHILDREN *sitting in class, among
them,* DAVID *(aged 8).
As we see this, we hear the voice of*

DAVID'S MUM:
You'll do us proud, David. We did sacri-
fice for you, saved up for you to go to the
Catholic School . . .

MISSIONARY:
White people. There is a high moral tone
to British people. From the very first days
of Britain . . . from the time of Runnymede . . .

At Home

DAVID'S DAD:
The Yoruba people, to whom the Oluwales belong,
are a very ancient race of people.

In Church

PREACHER:
The forces of light and brightness: those things
to which questing human nature gives its allegiance.
And those forces of darkness, of blackness, of evil.

David's Mum's Place

DAVID'S MUM *and* DAVID (*aged 14*)

DAVID'S MUM:
No one will ever get very far in these parts. But
if ever you can get to the white man's part of the
world . . .

Lagos City (night)

DAVID (*aged 16*), *is taking round*
SAILORS. *It is the mid-1940s.*

DAVID:
So now we reach the red-light area . . .

A Night-club

A SAILOR *leans back as he sits at a
table at which sit* DAVID *and other*
SAILORS.

SAILOR:
It's nothing on Aden.

The Waterfront

A group of young BLACKS *sit watching
the ships go out. Among them* DAVID
(*now 18*), *singing a song from the late
'40s. The song continues as we hear the
voices of the following;*

DAVID:
Mum, what would you say if I went over to
England?

MUM:
Oh, David, that would be wonderful.
 (*pause*)

BLACK:
Pigs. Pigs. Pigs to the slaughter in a way.
Some of them were very defenceless, naive.
You know, wanting the big time.

Nightclub

BLACK:
They tell me, you know, that the white man's
world is the ideal place.
Better than this place.
We should go over to the white man's part of
the world,
where the good things are.

Nightclub

Round a table are grouped a RICH
CRUISER *and two* CRUISING FRIENDS.
And DAVID.

RICH CRUISER:
Britain. Oh it's rather fun, you know.

Nightclub

BLACK:
You can have a good time in Britain
which you can't have back home because, you
know . . .
Well, here there are so many Muslims
from very strict background.

A House in Lagos

We see a typical Lagos house and a
family sit eating outside it.
The voice of a

BLACK:
A ticket to Britain cost £50.
It was better to stow away than pay £50.
Fifty quid out there means you can buy a house.

Various Shots

We see various stills of £50 houses
in Lagos.
Most of them have life going on
around them, i.e. families sit on
doorsteps, etc.

BLACK:
Fifty pound will buy you a maid for four or five
years.

A Street

Two CHILDREN *are playing a typical*
game in the streets of Lagos.

A Bar

Two BLACKS *stand by the bar, talking.*

FRIEND:
David's going to England.

BARMAN:
David going to England! Is he?

BLACK:
No! That's good! Then we'll see some action!

BLACK:
Wow! When David's got to England . . . !

David's Home

MUM:
We did sacrifice for you to go to the
Catholic School,
spent money on you.
Now you can repay us.

Another Bar

DAVID *and two* FRIENDS.

FRIEND:
Easy. We can easy get you on the ship.

David's Mum's Place

DAVID:
(*nonchalantly*) Well goodbye Mum. See you.

MUM:
(*weeping*) Goodbye David.

DAVID:
(*nonchalantly*) See you around, Mum.

ON THE WAY TO BRITAIN

On Board the Temple Star

The voice of a
BLACK:
David stowed away on board the *Temple Star*
on August 16th, 1949.

*Camera wanders round the
ship till we're close to* DAVID*'s
hiding place.*

The voice of a
WEST INDIAN:
Nigerians weren't the only ones coming to
Britain in them days.
There was a crowd of us, many West Indian men
came on the *Empire Windrush*.

We see a WHITE *standing by
the open door of* DAVID*'s hiding place.*

WHITE:
Hey, look at this, Fred. Fred, we got a
stowaway here.
DAVID *comes out, shamefacedly.*

WHITE:
Oh no, not another? Who's going to tell old
Willie?
(*pause*)

On Board: the Bridge

WHITE *has just told* CAPTAIN *the news*

CAPTAIN:
(*wearily*) All right, tell him we'll turn him
in when we get to Britain.

IN BRITAIN

In a British Black Drinking Club

BLACK:
Twenty-eight days in a British nick—
that's the price of a ticket from Lagos.
It's quite all right for blacks to come to
Britain.
The only crime is stowaway.

BLACK:
One day, of course, they may . . .

BLACK:
What, stop us coming? No, they can't do that
at all . . .

Various Shots

Trains of BLACKS *arrive in British
stations. Faces of hostile* WHITES.

MAUREEN:
It was a shock for many of them when they
arrived.
They had been taught to think of the white
man's country
as a father figure.
But when they got here the father figure
was a rejecting father figure.

CAPTAIN:
We've arrived in England as you see.
I'm going to send a message to the police now
to come to pick you up.

DAVID:
It is only twenty-eight days in nick?

WHITE:
Only twenty-eight days.
Actually, if you're good, it will only be
twenty-one days.
But it will be twenty-one days to remember.

PRISON

In Court

DAVID *stands listening in the dock as the*
MAGISTRATE *says:*

MAGISTRATE:
You will go to prison . . .

In Prison: Reception Area

DAVID *is having a shower*

PRISON OFFICER:
All right! Let's have you!

Prison Cell

Studies of pin-ups.
We see DAVID *and* TWO OTHERS *sitting*
beneath pin-ups, listless.
Music.

Exercise Yard, and other Prison Locations

Brief studies of DAVID *in the nick.*

Prison Reception Area

DAVID's *stint in prison is over. He*
is being given back his clothes.

PRISON OFFICER:
There you are. So what will you do now, black man?

DAVID:
Have a good time, white man.

HAPPY DAYS

Mecca Dance Hall

Late forties music and decor.
DAVID *dances, admired by* FRIENDS.

BLACK:

But David Oluwale, what a man!
His jitterbugging and rumba dancing!
He was only a little bloke but with that
he put us all in his pocket.

BLACK:

Clothes.
Them days David wore them snap brim
Trilbys,
and the draped zoot suits what the folks
were wearing at that time.

BLACK:

In those days there were less than a hundred
Africans in town,
so we used to meet regular,
and especially in the Mecca ballroom.
And in the clubs.

Black Drinking Club (night)

*We see studies of a typical black
drinking club as we hear*

BLACK:

There is two, no, three, four types of lovely
women that go to the club.
(These clubs they have names like, Caribbean

Club, International Club, you know, Pan
African Club.)
Four types of women.
First there is the coloured girls that have gone
and escaped from their homes.
They won't stay in the club long,
their mothers will soon come
and take them back
and give them a bollocking.
Then there's a few coloured girls that are on
the game.
You know, prostitutes.
Then there's the young white girls. To them,
the black man is something exciting.
To see these white girls, they often dress
in white chiffon, white lace, something
like that.
They are really lovely girls: and really
young.
The black man sends them wild.
Ah, there's many fights among the young white
girls about the black man.
And the last, there is the older type of
English woman,
the type that is just right, mature, man.
Real women.
Englishmen maybe they don't look round to look
at them.
But to the black man they are the most
beautiful of all.
Wonderful British women.

BLACK:
This crazy jitterbugging man, David!

DAVID, *up at the microphone, sings.*

BLACK:

He gives the good time song, the good time word.
He know how to make a party really swing.

DAVID:

(*in time to the music*) Just please me, baby,
oo ah oo!
Just please me baby, oo ah oo!
Just please me baby!

BLACK:

Does David have a woman?

BLACK:

David has a woman. Well!
You have to have a woman!

BLACK:

Her name is Gladys.

BLACK:

(*gloating*) Gladys . . .

We see GLADYS *dancing with* DAVID.
The camera remains mainly on GLADYS.
Meanwhile we hear the voice of a

BLACK:

Gladys, as far as is known is alive today.
Although the searches of Scotland Yard and
the local C.I.D.,
A court case,
Many solicitors' clerks
And many journalists have failed to find her.
She's lying low.
Wise woman.
She's somewhere in Britain now,
With her two children that David had by her,
Who by now must be aged about eighteen and
twenty.

At the bar of the club we now
see a

GAMBLING BLACK:
We used to do quite a bit of gambling.
David was there.
We played at my house mainly.

The weekend gambling party in
Gambling Black's Pad. DAVID *and three*
BLACKS *are present*

GAMBLING BLACK:
We'd start after work on Fridays,
Carry on until Sunday night.
The boys liked to play with me,
Because when I won I would always give them back
a pound.
For them to get home.
I wouldn't turn them out with nothing.
I've always been lucky with dice.
I know how to make the dice
Sound as if I'm shaking it in my hand
When really I'm not.
I can get the six often to go time after
time,
But I can't do it with both the dice.
I've always been lucky because
I can have the edge over them, these boys.
It's like when *I* meet the big people of the
gambling world:
Then *I* don't stand a chance.

At Another Black Club

Lounging at a bar, two other blacks take up
the story.

BLACK:
We used to cook up rice at these weekend
gambling parties.
A bit of curry.
A lot of cups of coffee.

BLACK:
David always drank . . . a lot of coffee.

In a Pub

DAVID *is sitting alone with a half
pint of bitter.*

BLACK:
Cheer up man! Hey, cheer up!
I always see you sit here in the pub.

BLACK:
Yes man, what are you doing? Sitting all
alone?

DAVID *thinks carefully before he replies.*

DAVID:
Same as any man else, I suppose.
Get away from the wife and the children.

BLACK:
You got children?

DAVID:
Yeah, sure.
Got two children.

The Brickworks

DAVID *is clocking in for work at the
local brickworks.
He carries a briefcase.*

BLACK:
David always carried with him a briefcase.
And that briefcase was filled with papers.
Educated papers.
David was always reading.

We see DAVID *at work at the brickworks.*

BLACK:
Me. I am a man of no education.
But David, he was a man with a deep respect
for education.
And he came to England to study.
He wanted to be an engineer.

We see DAVID *studying an engineering
manual, during teabreak.*

BLACK:
We had to stick close in those days.
It was always hard to find a job.
Or a place to live.
So we help each other out.

Outside a House

DAVID *stands talking to a* LANDLADY.

BLACK:
We go looking for a room.
A white woman collapses when she sees us
standing in front of her.
She's not seen a black man before!

A Street at night

DAVID *walking home.*
TWO POLICEMEN *approach him and begin
to question him.*

BLACK:

The police were the biggest problem.
Yeah, whatever we did they would stop us.
Two or three times on one single walk between
the city centre and where we lived,
And especially at night.
If we said: 'Why do this?'
they run us in for obstruction or something.
Then they charge us with something bigger;
Drugs or assault.

Outside another House

DAVID *is talking to another* LANDLADY.

BLACK:

When we went to look for rooms,
They would slam the doors, the whites.
I've been in many countries,
Zambia, Ghana, Nigeria, many places.
I never met other people who would do that.
And then the law . . .

BLACK:

The police . . .
The trouble is . . .
Have no idea the way we live.

In a Black Club

BLACK:

Yes, the police may be lacking in understanding.
White people they go to bed at eleven or twelve.
But the black man, that's when the night
begins.
He likes to be out in the clubs or having
parties.

In a Municipal Office

WHITE:

Such parties are frequently rowdy,
Causing offence to neighbours.
And at some there is illegal trading
In Liquor, off licensed premises;
Which, of course, we have to stamp on hard.

In a Black Club

DAVID *is sitting with some* FRIENDS.

MAUREEN:

Unpleasant.
We would be in the club.
In come, say,
Nine policemen.

MAUREEN *is a white who is friendly
to blacks. We see what
she describes.*

MAUREEN:

First thing they do,
They tell them to turn off the music.
Then go up to a table
Where a black is sitting with his friends.

POLICEMAN:

We'd like a word with you,
Sir, outside.

The club lights go up.

DAVID:

What about here?

BLACK:

Well sure, but why not here?

POLICEMAN:

Never mind about here.
We want to see you outside.

MAUREEN:

He's with his friends.
And has that scene going.
And he doesn't want to go.
But at length he goes outside with them.

DAVID *goes outside with the policemen.*

Outside the Club

POLICEMAN:

We're making enquiries
In connection with the theft of some metal.

MAUREEN:

It turns out that they believe him
To be someone different to who he is.

DAVID:

Stop wasting my time.

DAVID *turns to go back to the club.*

MAUREEN:

He begins to return to the club.
The policemen stand in his way.
He brushes his arm against the policemen
As he goes past.
Next thing he finds himself being charged
With the assault of a policeman.

At the Police Station

POLICEMAN:

If you plead guilty
We'll let you out tonight.

POLICEMAN:
If you plead not guilty
You'll be remanded in custody until the trial.

There is a long silence. Then DAVID *says:*

DAVID:
I agree. I am guilty.

MAUREEN:
And it appears on his records 'Assault of a
police constable'.
And from then on he's a marked man.

In a Pentecostal Church

A Pentecostal Service is in progress.
Over the sound of the singing we hear the
voice of

WHITE:
The coloured people are still very religious,
More than the whites.
Many of the coloured community still go
To church on a Sunday,
To the various churches they have,
Including 'Pentecostal Churches'.

He says this last with disdain.

A Rubbish Tip

Two BLACKS *with a rubbish disposal*
vehicle. They are unloading it.

BLACK:
Why did the black man come here?
Who caused it?

BLACK:
Was it the priests who painted the picture
of a glorious Britain?

In Church

DAVID *smiling amid the singing congregation.*

FAMILY LIFE

A Street

DAVID *holds* GLADYS'*s hand as they*
walk down it.
They reach a terrace house.
DAVID *reaches through letter-box for the key.*

GLADYS:
I went to the fortune-telling machine.
It says: 'An ordinary house in a street like any
other,
Will one day be for you the most wonderful
place in the world.'

DAVID *opens the door and they are greeted*
by their CHILDREN, *and white* BABY-
SITTER.

Outside a Neighbour's House

MRS. WHITE:
David was an ordinary man.
He lived down the street with Gladys and the kids.

At the Brickworks

DAVID *is working. We hear the voice of*

MRS. WHITE:
He worked with my husband in the West Yorkshire
Foundries.

In a Neighbour's House

DAVID *is baby-sitting*

       MRS. WHITE:
David liked children.
Sometimes he'd baby-sit for ours.

BACK TO THE NICK

In Magistrates Court

CLERK:
The charge is that you obstructed P. C. Brown in
the execution of his duty.
And secondly that you did assault him.
Do you understand the charge?

DAVID:
Yes.

CLERK:
Do you plead guilty or not guilty?

DAVID:
(*wearily*) Guilty.

In Magistrates Court: later

MAGISTRATE:
It must be clearly understood that assault
Of a policeman is a grave charge.
You will go to prison for three months.

Prison Reception Area

DAVID *and three* OTHERS *are received
into prison by* PRISON OFFICERS.

Prison

Studies of DAVID'*s life
in prison. We hear the voice of a*

BLACK:

It was David's second prison sentence,
four years after his arrival,
for assaulting a police officer
that, many claim, was the start of his downfall.
And there are those who say that because
assault is easy to prove,
and that getting a number of convictions
is the sign of a zealous policeman,
some police may have erred into provoking members
of the new black settlers into assault.
At that time, many towns in Britain
were having problems about getting used to these
new settlers.
A long time later, a policeman who was convicted
of assault on David was sent to that same prison
that David went to;
and his wife, a different sort of woman to David's
Gladys,
became concerned at what she saw when she visited
him . . .

Inspector's Home

INSPECTOR'S WIFE:

. . . What I saw at the prison appalled me.
It is one of the most terrible places on God's
earth,
and I would not wish the vilest creature living
to be detained there.
It's fit for rats and not human beings.

Prison Waiting-room

INSPECTOR'S WIFE and OTHER WIVES
are in the waiting-room.

INSPECTOR'S WIFE:
I'll never forget it.
We visitors were ushered into a waiting-room;
and packed in like sheep.
They are waiting.
SHE *and two* PEOPLE *with her light
cigarettes.*

PRISON OFFICER:
(*sharply*) No smoking.

Prison Passage

INSPECTOR'S WIFE *is led down a passage-way
that has cells on either side.*

INSPECTOR'S WIFE:
In one of the cells I saw a man sat on a low bed.
I have never in my life seen anyone look so
despondent.

They go on till they reach a small room.

Small Room

*In it is a table which has been
hastily wiped, but is still smeared
with dust.
There is one chair at one side and
there are three at the other.
The* INSPECTOR *is brought in,
he looks very unkempt.
His* WIFE *rises to greet him but is
motioned to sit down. Freeze.*

Prison. Various Shots

*Now we see studies of
DAVID's life in prison.*

NARRATOR:
What happened to David in this same prison?
Who knows?
Only Gladys perhaps knows,
and Gladys, if she's watching now,
will doubtless wisely keep quiet,
as she's done through it all.
The children know perhaps.
They too will remain silent.
All *we* know is that the man who was sane enough
for the court
to deal with him by sending him to prison in
April 1953,
was by the time he emerged from it in June,
mad enough for him to be discharged
to Psychiatric Hospital.

BLACK:
Something has happened to David.

A Municipal Chamber

Round a table sit MAUREEN *and* OTHER
WITNESSES.
And the Select Committee: MR. DEEDES
in the chair, MR. ARTHUR BOTTOMLEY,
Mr. NORMAN FOWLER, SIR GEORGE
SINCLAIR, MR. WILLIAM WILSON.
There is a small AUDIENCE, *mainly
witnesses who will be called later.*

BLACK:
The relationship between black
and white
is still of concern in the town where David died.
A select committee was convened to study
this relationship.

39

MAUREEN *is speaking. As well as being*
a liberal white,
she runs an organization designed
to produce better understanding between
blacks and whites.

MAUREEN:

Some criticisms which have been communicated to
the police by my organization:
1. Police are slow to come when an immigrant calls them.
They respond quickly to calls from indigenous
people.
2. The police have sometimes taken coloured
people unjustly when disturbance has occurred,
even though they were innocent, and the guilty
white people have made their escape.
3. Sometimes more force than necessary has been
used on coloured people.
4. The police have a habit of prodding West
Indians when speaking to them,
it has been alleged, deliberately,
as they know that West Indians are particularly
averse to this.
The police say in reply that they get the same
sort of complaints from the
indigenous people.
But consider the number and quality of
'discretionary charges'
made against black settlers.
These are usually charges of assaulting policemen, or disorderly conduct,
which are very easy to prove technically
and in the present climate of public opinion
may prove
very easy to get conviction on.

Such charges are extremely difficult to disprove
and, in my own experience,
leave the black settler in no doubt that
the police,
having failed through enquiry to establish
grounds for an arrest on the original or
alleged offence,
create a situation arising from which it is
only too easy
to make a charge of assault and gain a conviction.

The Municipal Chamber (later)

*Round the table there now sit as
witnesses a* SIKH, A PAKISTANI, A
WEST INDIAN, A MUSLIM, MR. NOEL,
and the Select Committee.

A SIKH:
Our temple is next door to the police
station and whenever we want help the
policeman is there.

MR. BOTTOMLEY:
Would members of the Sikh community want to
join the police?

SIKH:
We have lived in Kenya where our parents,
brothers, cousins and so on, have been in
the police force.
They used to be the major part of the Kenya
police force.

MR. BOTTOMLEY:
You have always provided a great number of
people
for the armed services in the Indian sub-
continent?

SIKH:
Yes.

MR. BOTTOMLEY:
Do you think that some initiative lies with
your community
to encourage some of your strapping young
people
to volunteer for service with the police?

SIKH:
In fact there are a few.
Not here but in London.
There are a few people who have made an
approach.
They were not up to the necessary standards.
They did make an attempt to join.

MR. BOTTOMLEY:
Suppose the police authorities were to say
they must not wear a turban,
would that cause a problem?

SIKH:
Yes, it would.
This is a religious matter.
They will not take off their turbans.

SIR GEORGE SINCLAIR:
No doubt your community will cite the
example
of the Royal Navy during the war,
our Senior Service welcomed blue turbans.

SIKH:

Thank you.

The Municipal Chamber (later)

A PAKISTANI:

A year ago there was a lot of breaking
of windows in the Burleigh Road area.
I took the matter up with the police,
and it was stopped.
Again, it was reported that Pakistani
people
were chased as they were coming from work at
night.
The matter was taken up with the police
who put extra patrols on,
and it was stopped.
Last year there was a problem of some
Pakistanis and Indians
going home at 10 o'clock,
who were chased by hooligans,
and stones thrown.
The police came and the matter was stopped.

An INDIAN *rises.*

INDIAN:

Our experience is the reverse.
It is a common practice with the law
offenders
to seek abode and refuge in slums and
socially deprived areas,
and, therefore, he who hails from that
locality
is looked down upon and is suspected of
all the nefarious activities.
Since, unfortunately, a majority
of our Indian people live in these shady

43

areas
out of no choice of their own,
the police label them, ipso facto,
as the law-breakers.
In this context I can state unequivocally
that the Indian residents here
are the most law-abiding citizens,
who are always imbued with a sense of
responsibility
towards the society in which they live.
They have not forgotten their age-old
tradition
of not breaking an established order.
It is our experience that the police
cannot see eye to eye with our people
residing together or moving out in groups.
We feel that the police have formed an
erroneous judgment
if they pre-suppose that such group
is tantamount to sedition or rebellious
attitude.
Apart from maintaining law and order
the police in this country is portrayed
here and abroad
as a social service agency,
but we regret to point out that in actual
practice,
it is anything but a helping organ.
We have been forced to reach this conclusion
when we witness so much of indifference
almost amounting to callousness
and a lack of sympathetic attitude
on the part of the police.

The Municipal Chamber (later)

A MUSLIM:

The police do not have the confidence of
the Muslims.
The distrust of the police now created
will remain
unless something is done fairly quickly.
Muslims need to feel that their culture
is understood by the police.
Perhaps it would help if social functions
could take place between the police
and the immigrant black man.

We see reactions of POLICEMEN
in the AUDIENCE *to this.*

The Municipal Chamber (later)

A WEST INDIAN:

We live here,
this is our home now,
but just looking out of our front door,
it reminds us West Indians of a perfect
police state.
Despite all the meetings and discussions
with senior officers,
intimidations and wrongful arrests go on
all the time;
black teenagers returning from Youth Centres
to their homes are jostled by the police,
and when the youth protests,
police reinforcements with dogs are always
ready just around corners.
As a result, arrests are always made.
Black immigrants are very often frightened
into giving information by false arrests.

Police boot and fist into compelling them
to give wrong statements,
but the right one the police require.
Lies are often made to look like truth,
and very often truth is made to look like
lies.
The majority of black people in this
area are working-class.
Shift work is common.
Can't a black immigrant leave his home at
5.30 a.m. to catch a bus without
being questioned and jostled by the police?
Can't he visit his friends and return at
11 p.m. or 12 p.m.
without being taken to the police station
for questioning?

> MR. NOEL *rises. He is a militant*
> BLACK *from elsewhere. There is now*
> *quite a high level of muttered*
> *comment at the meeting of the Select*
> *Committee.*

MR. NOEL:
Police do not have any respect at all for
black people.
It is often as though they are dealing
with a black animal.
In fact you will be surprised to hear me
say that I have been called
nigger from the forest,
a black hooligan.

MR. BOTTOMLEY:
Why have you not complained?

MR. NOEL:
The complaints procedure consists of
policemen.
We should appoint immigrants who could
understand immigrants,
West Indians, black people who can understand
black people.
You will never understand because you do
not want to.
Even round this table, many of you do not
want to.
Your system is your system and you have
no intention
of altering it to suit other people.
Maybe you would like to see us water down a
lot of things people are saying,
but the real factor is when you are there
and the police kick you around.
I know it! I have seen it!
It happens every day and nobody on this
table is prepared to tell you the real truth!

SIR GEORGE SINCLAIR:
Yes but, er, did you submit a memorandum on
this subject?

There is uproar.

TO THE BIN

Prison: Prison Welfare Officer's Office

The P.W.O. is speaking into the phone.

P.W.O.:
Yes, he's completely nuts. I don't know. No, it
happened while he was in here I think.
We'll have to send him to you. Alright.
I'll send a couple of officers down with him.

Psychiatric Hospital

*We see studies of life in Psychiatric Hospital.
Meanwhile we hear the voice of a friend of
David.*

BLACK:
When I went to the nuthouse I was amazed.
I never knew there were so many black men
there.
It made me sad.
And many with their hair grown long and
beards.
And when I got back to town and told them I
had seen David,
people asked me, David?
David there? David in the nuthouse?
How did he get like this?
It is difficult to say because
all these things are never talked about.
See what I mean?
One thing I know for sure.

David was not a drinking man.
He used to drink only half a pint of bitter.
Not a drinking man.

Now, as we see something of DAVID'S *life
in the bin, we hear other comments.*

WHITE:

He was at times withdrawn and at other
times
aggressive, violent and disturbed.
He saw lions with fishes' heads,
and said they were going to kill him and eat him.
He kicked, he struck, he hit, scratched,
and spat in people's faces.

MAUREEN:

The prison authorities had delivered David
to the mental hospital
where he was to remain for eight years.
David was twenty-two.
He had sixteen years to live.

A Park

A BLACK *talks to us as he sits in a park.*

BLACK:

People had been telling me he'd gone
crackers,
but bloody hell, I met him inside,
and he remembered me!
He knew exactly who I was!
So, well, that meant not potty,
because he remembered me.
There was nothing wrong with him, you know.
So we get to talk about where I come from,
where he come from,

and all the boys, all the boys he says about,
I know.
Yeah! All the Africans!
He knows them all!

Psychiatric Hospital

We see further studies of DAVID'S *life in
Psychiatric Hospital.*

WHITE:
Attempts to consult David's records of when he
was in Psychiatric Hospital,
or to speak with those who looked after him there,
have so far met with polite refusal.

HOSPITAL OFFICIAL:
I saw him in hospital and found him
to be childish, giggling,
talking in a confused manner,
and could not give a clear account of
himself.
He had no idea of the day or date,
and he had no true appreciation of
his condition.
He complained about the police,
he complained about the National Health
authorities,
he said he had been persecuted.
When he was initially admitted to the
hospital
he would defecate and urinate
on the ward floor
and in corners.

WHITE:
In 1959 came the Mental Health Act.
It recommends that those in Psychiatric
Hospital
who are deemed not dangerous and capable
of living outside
should be returned to their families or
live in small permissive hostels.
For this reason, or for some other,
it was decided that David should be
released.

A Street

DAVID *walks down a crowded street.*
He is free again.

DAVID BECOMES A DOSSER

A Public Park

DAVID *is sleeping on a park
bench.*

BLACK:

I tell you one thing, if I were going to
be a vagrant,
I wouldn't be a vagrant in this country
anyway.
If he was a vagrant in the country where
we come from, Africa,
we have a custom.
If a stranger comes and he has nowhere to go,
I will take him in my bed,
and he will eat my food . . .

The Public Park (later)

DAVID *is now sitting on the bench
and a* BLACK *is talking to him.*

BLACK:

But why?
Why do you not want to live in a house?
Go back to Gladys?

DAVID *looks at him sadly for a while
and then says*

DAVID:

Gladys won't have me.
There is another pause and then

BLACK:
David, you have changed.

A Street

We see DAVID *shambling around in an
old raincoat
with layers of underclothing to keep
him warm.
He carries his briefcase.
We cut to the trial that is to come in the*

Crown Court

WHITE *is giving evidence.*

WHITE:
A revolting figure;
stinking, dirty, and foul-mouthed.

Crown Court (later)

INSPECTOR:
I can only describe him as an animal,
not a human being.

A Club

MAUREEN:
He needed a long time to explain himself.
Once he had confidence in you he *would* talk.

Another Club

BLACK:
Two things caused his breakdown.
The end of his relationship with his woman;
and the realization that he was not going
to succeed.

In a Club

BLACK:
You can't go back if you fail.
Because you feel you've failed not only
yourself,
but your relations too.

ANOTHER BLACK:
Yes, because when we stowed away and came
to England,
it was a big thing.
People out in Lagos said: 'When he comes back it
will be *great*.
Then we'll see some *action*.'
And if you've failed you feel you have to hide.
Maybe that's why he couldn't return.
To leave and come to Britain is a gamble.
Either you win it all,
or you lose it all.

THE WORLD OF DOSSHOUSES

We see studies of typical
common lodging houses as we hear

WHITE:
At this point in his life David needed care.
But where could he go?
The Mental Health Act (1959) directed that
patients like him, sick but not dangerous,
should be discharged into 'community care'—
the Local Health Service.
The Royal Commission on Mental Health, on
which the Act was based
had recommended that Local Authorities
provide special hostels for patients.
Most—including David's home town—did.
But they were not built in large enough
numbers
and those that were built were not suitable
for mentally abnormal vagrants
who eschew organized assistance.
The Welfare State gave David money—up to
£3 14s. a week—
with which he bought food and a few beers.
But it did not provide accommodation of
the type he needed.
Some years before, the official government
centre for vagrants
had been closed in this town.
Along with hundreds of others up and down
the country.
An official policy of what was known as

enquiry and questioning
had also resulted in a reduction of the
vagrant population.
The nearest Government Reception Centre
was now ten miles away in another town.
It has since been replaced by a new one.

OFFICIAL WHITE:
It is a posh place.

WHITE:
But the standards of entry and hygiene
of the existing one
were already too severe for such as David.
What else was there?

Salvation Army Hostel

*We see exterior of a large
Hostel.*

WHITE:
In hostels like this accommodation is
provided.
David stayed there.
An officer stands in the doorway.

OFFICER:
Bed-wetting, vermin-carrying, drunkenness,
and being late,
all carry risk of expulsion from our places.
You must know that.

WHITE:
In the end, David was blacklisted.

Church Army Hostel

*We see a smaller
Hostel.*

WHITE:
In the Church Army Hostel he found a home
for three months.
But men are turned out of this place
if they have made no attempt to find a job,
or are otherwise unsatisfactory.

A Derelict Building

DAVID *prepares to sleep.*

WHITE:
David began to sleep in shop doorways
and 'hot spots' like the local brickworks,
and next to the steam pipes that emerged
under the railway arches,
such as those near the river
where later he met his death.

In Magistrates Court

WHITE:
A few months after release from the Psychiatric
Hospital,
David was again in court.

CLERK:
Offence—malicious wounding of a policeman.

Magistrates Court (later)

MAGISTRATE:
I sentence you to six months.

In Magistrates Court

We see DAVID *in court again.*

WHITE:
Within the next two years he was again
sentenced.

MAGISTRATE:
One month, for disorderly conduct.
A fortnight for drunk and disorderly.

Foyer of Prison

We see DAVID *being discharged.*

Psychiatric Hospital

We see DAVID *once more in Psychiatric Hospital.*

WHITE:
In 1965, after being again charged with
assaulting a constable,
he was again committed to Psychiatric Hospital.
He was again discharged.

Public Park

DAVID *sits.*

WHITE:
Friends in the black community used to see
him
sitting on park benches—a forlorn figure.

Probation Office

DAVID *sits at desk opposite* MARY.

MARY:
But for any man who really wants to go back to
Africa, there exist funds to find him
the price of a ticket!

DAVID:

Er . . . eh . . . er . . .

He continues to mumble.

WHITE:

David at one time nearly agreed to accept
this money and go.
If only he had.
If only he had.

Freeze for a moment on DAVID'S *face.*

In a Club

BLACK:

(*excitable*) I'll tell you something about
David Oluwale.
He was Yoruba.
Yes.
Yoruba, they're shrewd.
First the Ibo, they come first, then the
Yoruba.
Very intelligent.
I'll tell you one thing I'd like to
find.
Oluwale's briefcase.
When they found him in the river, they say his
pockets were filled with jewellery.
He was a shrewd man.
They are the brains of Africa.
Like Jewish people.
The Ibo or the Yoruba that can take up this cup
and sell it and buy something else.
They can make a penny turn into a pound.
And they know more about white people, more than
the Ghanains or the Gambians.
They use them to grow rich.

Oh yes, I'd like to know where David Oluwale's
briefcase is.

Freeze for a moment on his face.

Outside Dwelling House

MRS. WHITE:
David did still work occasionally;
at one time I saw him sweeping up leaves.
One thing that really puzzled my husband and me,
was that David was really frightened of water,
and spoke to my husband about this fear,
more than once.

Outside a Shop

MRS. WHITE:
He used to sleep outside here,
which I used to clean at.
We used to tell him to move on,
when we arrived for the morning clean.
He'd waken up,
gather his belongings,
and go away.
He was better than most men are,
at that time of day!

In a Park

DAVID *sits*.
We see his face in close up.

BLACK:
Has a man the right to live in whatever
way he chooses?
Has he the right to die in whatever way
he chooses?
It was now 1965,
and David had four more years to live.

MORE VISITS TO THE NICK

In Crown Court

Now we are again looking forward to the
court case that followed David's death.

WHITE:
A terrifying figure.
A type who may suddenly spring from the
shadows,
and assault you.

In a Street

WHITE:
He had a physique of a Charles Atlas.

In a Pub

BLACK:
I remember his smile.

BLACK:
Then, his gentleness.

BLACK:
Third, he was so solitary.

In a Club

WHITE:
And he was a small quiet man.

Prison Reception Area

BLACK:
Now David's visits to prison became more
frequent.

DAVID *stands handing his clothes
in.*

BLACK:
August 1967.

PRISON OFFICER *is checking through
his files.*

PRISON OFFICER:
David Oluwale: 28 days.
Offence: wandering abroad.
Date of discharge: 23rd September, 1967.

Prison

Studies of DAVID'S *life in
prison.*

WHITE:
About 50,000 people are discharged in the course
of a year
from the prisons of England and Wales.
Probably at least 10,000 are homeless.
When the gates close behind them, no one knows
(and few care)
whether they will turn to the right or to the left.
What *is* known is that most of them will soon
be back.
And while it costs us over £1,000 a year to
keep a man in prison,
to say nothing of the cost of his crime,
we provide only minimal resources to help

keep him out of prison once he leaves it.
Too many fall back into criminal ways.

David's Cell

BLACK:
A visit from the Prison Welfare Officer.

P.W.O.:
Will you be remaining in town?

DAVID:
Yes.

P.W.O.:
Will you be seeking your own accommodation?

DAVID:
Yes.

P.W.O.:
Do you have a job to go to?

DAVID:
No.

Prison Reception Area

DAVID *is receiving back his clothes.*

In a Park

DAVID *is sighted by* TWO POLICE-MEN *who begin to follow him.*

WHITE:
A fortnight or so after that he was back inside
again,
again on this somewhat archaic charge—
'wandering abroad'.

Prison Reception Area

DAVID *stands, handing in his clothes.*

BLACK:

October 1967.
We hear the voices of the

CLERK:

Wandering abroad.

MAGISTRATE:

56 days.

BLACK:

Date of discharge: 1st December, '67.

Solicitor's Office

SOLICITOR:

What is this crime of 'wandering abroad'?
It comes from the Vagrancy Act of 1824.
'An Act for the punishment of idle and disorderly
persons, and rogues and vagabonds . . .
be it . . . enacted that every person
wandering abroad and lodging in any barn or
outhouse,
or any deserted or unoccupied building,
or in the open air, or under a tent,
or in any cart or wagon,
not having any visible means of subsistence,
and not giving a good account of himself
or herself . . .
shall be deemed a rogue and vagabond . . .

Magistrates Court

BLACK:

A little later David was back again.
January, 1968.

CLERK:
Wandering abroad. Indecent exposure.

Magistrates Court (later)

MAGISTRATE:
56 days. 3 months consecutive.

BLACK:
Effective duration 146 days.
Date of discharge: 29th March, '68.

Solicitor's Office

SOLICITOR:
Indecent exposure sounds bad until we learn
that it can be used to describe those who urinate
in public places, even though after dark.

Back Entrance of Magistrates Court

DAVID *enters court from police car.*

BLACK:
Two weeks after discharge
he was in court again,
for disorderly conduct.

In Magistrates Court

MAGISTRATE:
We're taking a lenient view.
I'm giving you a suspended sentence.

Probation Office

MARY *and* DAVID. MARY *is writing.*

MARY:

17th April, '68. Mr. Oluwale has been in court
this morning for disorderly conduct.
He was given a conditional discharge, and
produced an order.

MARY:

Where were you sleeping?
Until arrested?

DAVID:

I have been sleeping in the entrance of John Peters
Limited.

MARY:

Have you recently received anything from the
Social Security?

DAVID:

Yes, from Merrion Street, on last Friday.

MARY:

I wonder if we can get you in the Church
Army?
> *She phones the Army Hostel and*
> *explains the situation. We can't*
> *hear what she says.*

MARY:

The captain will accept you.

Church Army Hostel

DAVID *outside the door.*

C.A. CAPTAIN:

Mr. Oluwale?

DAVID:

(*grunts*)

C.A. CAPTAIN:

We have a place for you.

In Church Army Hostel

C.A. CAPTAIN *and* DAVID.

CAPTAIN:

Men are turned out of this place,
if they have made no attempt to find a job,
or are otherwise unsuitable. We have put you up
here before.
Now you . . .

A Derelict Building

DAVID *settles down to sleep.*

MARY:

A year later I was to try the Church Army
again,
and all the other hostels in town,
but by that time David had sunk.
He was no longer acceptable to them.

WHITE:

Blame should not necessarily be directed at
these organizations.
If only there were more of them, it might
be possible to find beds for every dosser—
not only the better behaved.

Prison

BLACK:
David went to prison again.
He was released in June.

A Public Park

DAVID *sits in a public park where
trees are blowing in the wind.*

WHITE:
It was not only in prison that David
suffered.
He was also subject to harassment
by those who object to vagrants in general,
and by two policemen in particular.

Stills Sequence
*As he speaks we see stills portraits
of two typical* POLICEMEN.

WHITE:
Both of these two men took pride in their
city and its police.
The sergeant was one of the few sergeants
in the Force
who still wore a helmet, not the more
fashionable peaked cap.
The Inspector was a tall dark-haired man.
Both wished to see their city a 'clean city',
and of course both were bound to see that
the law was not flouted,
including the stipulations of the Vagrancy
Act.
The Inspector's promising career came to
an end
when he tried to protect a superintendent

whose car had knocked down an old woman,
by saying he had smelt alcohol on her breath.
The woman was teetotal.
He went to prison—
the same prison that David so often went to.

Prison Cell

The INSPECTOR *sits, dejected.*

WHITE:
And while he was in prison rumours began
to circulate that he had been connected
with the harassment of David.

Crown Court

MR. JOHN COBB, Q.C.:
The case for the prosecution is that these
two accused persons
made it their business to make life
unpleasant for this man,
for they certainly did not want him
within the city boundaries.
They hounded and harassed him.
They teased him cruelly and made a torment
of his life.

Police Station

The INSPECTOR *receives a message
on the telephone. We hear* COBB'S
voice describe what followed.

COBB:
It became well known at their station
that if ever this man was sighted,
a message had to be passed through for
them to go out
and deal with him.

Crown Court

COBB:

At 3.30 on August 7th, '68,
a police constable looked inside the doorway
of a shop called the Bridal House
in the town centre,
and saw these two policemen and the Nigerian.
The Nigerian was shouting.

Bridal House (night)

*The Bridal House is a large store in whose
windows wedding dresses are displayed.
It has a wide porch, warmed with bright lights.*

DAVID:

Leave me alone!
I have to sleep somewhere!
Leave me alone!

Crown Court

COBB:

They were pushing him like a plaything,
backwards and forwards with the flat of
their hands.
He was clutching his duffle bag,
containing all his wordly possessions.
He fell.

Bridal House (night)

DAVID *is on his hands and knees
and the* INSPECTOR *and* SERGEANT *stand
over him*

INSPECTOR:

Get up! Get up!

70

COBB:
He was on his hands and knees,
and they kicked them away,
causing him to fall down.
The Inspector started to beat him
about the head and shoulders.
The Sergeant gave him a kick on the backside.

Bridal House (night)

As they kick and beat him, there
are grunts from DAVID. *He gets*
up and runs.

Crown Court

COBB:
The man escaped from the doorway and ran off.
At 4.20 a.m. the constable was again driving
past
when he saw the man being pursued by the
Inspector,
with the Sergeant some distance behind.

Bridal House (night)

P.C. SEAGER'S *car stands in the*
foreground. DAVID *is running*
towards us with the INSPECTOR *and*
SERGEANT *behind.*

INSPECTOR:
Get down there and stop him!
P.C. SEAGER *leaves his vehicle and*
goes towards DAVID.

Crown Court

COBB:

He saw the Inspector dive at the Nigerian,
as if to make a Rugby tackle,
and the two men crashed onto the roadway.

Street near Bridal House (night)

DAVID *is on the ground with the*
INSPECTOR *on top of him. The* SERGEANT
runs up and DAVID *is put in the police
car.*

In the Police Car (night)

SEAGER, INSPECTOR, SERGEANT *and*
DAVID *are travelling.*

DAVID:

Why don't you leave me alone? I have to sleep.

Crown Court

COBB:

He showed no resistance at that time.
P.C. Seager noticed that his face appeared
to be swelling under the left eye.
The Nigerian asked what was going to happen
to him.
The Inspector said that they were going
to take him for a cup of tea.

In the Police Car (night)

They are travelling, as before.

COBB:

The constable drove the Sergeant and the
Inspector and the Nigerian

out of the city altogether
to a village seven miles away.

A Village (night)

A Pub.
DAVID *stands beside the car.*

INSPECTOR:
See that building there?
It's a public house.
Knock on the door, they'll give you a
cup of tea.

The car drives off.
DAVID, *bewildered, moves towards
the pub.*

A Wood (night)

Long shot. DAVID *being pushed
from car by same* POLICEMEN.

COBB:
Later, the same team picked the Nigerian up
and drove him to some woods where they left him.

POLICEMAN:
Down in the jungle, where he belongs.

Civic Buildings

Imposing views of Civic Buildings.
Civic music.

MARY:
But it was because they wanted a clean city.
That's all.
They couldn't bear to have tramps
littering up their city.

73

St. Peters Crypt

A crypt filled with TRAMPS.
DAVID *has entered.*
WHITE TRAMPS *sitting there look
at him with hostility.*

The Street

SEAGER *is helping the* INSPECTOR
and the SERGEANT *put* DAVID *in a
police van.*
DAVID *is lashing out with his arms
but does not strike anyone.*

In the Van

The INSPECTOR *and the* SERGEANT *start
to hit* DAVID *with their feet and hands
about his head and shoulders.*

COBB:
Another policeman will say about this same
incident,
that after the Nigerian was in the van,
the two policemen started hitting him.

INSPECTOR:
He has bitten my thumb!

The SERGEANT *hits* DAVID *with a
torch. The glass breaks.*

At the Police Station

DAVID *at the Police Station. The*
INSPECTOR *is kicking him in the
crutch.
Blood is trickling from his mouth.
His eyes are wide open.
He appears terrified.*

In Crown Court

P.C. ATKINSON:
(*emotional*) Blows were struck to the Nigerian's
body and testicles.
I have never seen a man crying so much in
my life.
There was no noise but tears were going
down his face.
Many tears.

In the Police Station

DAVID *is now drooped across the*
counter.

INSPECTOR:
He's being charged with assaulting me.

Magistrates Court

PROSECUTION:
Two assaults on the Inspector,
one on the Sergeant, and one
charge for disorderly conduct.

Magistrates Court (later)

MAGISTRATE:
We find you guilty:
and sentence you to three months'
imprisonment.
There is also a suspended sentence of three
months to be brought into force,
so you'll serve a total of six months.
Have you anything to say?

DAVID:
(*has nothing to say*).

75

BLACK:
Date of discharge: 10th January, '69.

In David's Cell

DAVID *says to his cell mates.*

DAVID:
What's prison meant to do to you?
Make you better or make you worse?

Prison Doctor's Consulting Room

DOCTOR *and* ASSISTANT.

PRISON DOCTOR:
We'll have to make a change in that.
His medical category can no longer be referred
to as Grade A1. (*He makes notes.*)

WHITE:
Another change occurs in David's papers at
this time.
His date of birth has changed.
It now appears as 9th September, '29;
not 8th September, '30, as previously.
David has grown one year older.
Prison Welfare Officer's Report.

> *As* P.W.O. *talks to* DAVID *in prison
> he is writing his report.*

P.W.O.:
Several times in prison. He has been unemployed
some time.
Is of very low intelligence and I would think,
could be very aggressive,
and is going to have great difficulty
in staying out of trouble on release.

BLACK:
The Prison Welfare Officer was right.
Three days later:

In Magistrates Court

BLACK:
January 13th, '69.

CLERK:
Offence: disorderly conduct.

In Magistrates Court (later)

MAGISTRATE:
Sentence: 14 days.

BLACK:
Date of discharge: 23rd January, '69.

Outside Prison

DAVID *leaves the nick. We hear the Prison Welfare Officer's report.*

P.W.O.:
Many times in prison.
Has not worked for six months.
A labourer by trade but does not seem
to have done a lot of work.
No job to go to on release.

BLACK:
David had now three more months to live.
Three days later:

Police Station

*The inner door of the police
station bursts open.*

DAVID *is propelled through the*
doors and falls on the floor.
The SERGEANT *speaks to P.C. over*
the counter.
The INSPECTOR *follows him in and*
kicks him while he is on the floor.
We hear the voice of COBB.

COBB:

What kind of kick was it?

WOMAN P.C.:

It was a very hard kick.
A kick between the legs.
    The INSPECTOR *helps the* SERGEANT
    to lift the NIGERIAN *off the floor*
    and they drape him over the
    counter.
    As he is draped over the counter
    DAVID *is holding his private parts*
    with both his hands
    and he is crying.

Magistrates Court

BLACK:

January 27th, 1969.

CLERK:

Offence: disorderly conduct.

Magistrates Court (later)

MAGISTRATE:

Fourteen days.

BLACK:

Date of discharge: 5th February, '68.

Prison: David's Cell

The PRISON WELFARE OFFICER *is
talking to* DAVID *in his cell.*

BLACK:
Prison Welfare Officer's Report:

P.W.O.:
Only released a few days ago.
Unemployed, never worked.
Has no settled way of life—
No place to lodge when he is released.
Deteriorating all the time.
Difficult and unreasoning,
and gave no opportunity to talk out his
problems.

In David's Cell (later)

BLACK:
But why they do these things to you?

DAVID:
Something has gone wrong.

The Bridal House

We see the SERGEANT *urinating
over* DAVID *as he is lying in the
doorway.*

Magistrates Court

BLACK:
Two weeks later David was in prison again.
February, '69.

CLERK:
Offence: disorderly conduct.

Magistrates Court (later)

MAGISTRATE:
Fourteen days.

BLACK:
Date of discharge: 8th March, '69.

P.W.O.'s Office

P.W.O. *and* DAVID.

BLACK:
Prison Welfare Officer's Report.
The P.W.O. *is writing.*

P.W.O.:
Possibly if reasonable accommodation could be
found for him, it may help to keep him out
of prison.
I did wonder what help could be given him and
how he responded in the past.
The P.W.O. *looks up.*

P.W.O.:
Would you like assistance to find accommodation on release?

DAVID *mumbles, then sits back and
gazes mutely at* P.W.O.

Outside Probation Office

DAVID *approaches Probation Officer*

BLACK:
David's name appears again on the official
files,
in the record of when he called at the city's
probation office
three days after his next release on
11th March.

In the Probation Office

DAVID *and* MARY *sit opposite one another.*

MARY:
He was hard to understand and scruffy.

MARY:
Where have you been sleeping?

DAVID:
Sleeping rough.

MARY:
Do you need a bed for the night?

DAVID:
Yes, bed for the night. And I . . .
(*unintelligible*)

MARY:

What?

DAVID:

(*unintelligible*)

We see MARY *lift the phone and
hear her voice comment.*

MARY:
I tried two Salvation Army Hostels,
the Church Army Hostel,
and the Shaftesbury Hostel,

but discovered that David was now blacklisted
at every one I tried.

In the Probation Office (later)

MARY:
Do you want to go home to Nigeria?

MARY:
How would you pay for your fare?

MARY:
Would you like me to try to help you?

*We see MARY again lift the
phone and hear her voice comment.*

MARY:
I rang the M.O.S.S. and they informed me
that there is a scheme but he must make
application.
I began to explain this to him.

In the Probation Office (later)

MARY:
Excuse me, if you go about it the right
way,
your fare back home *can* be paid.

*MARY looks at DAVID and there
is a long silence. At length it
seems that he is about to speak.*

DAVID:
No good.

*Slowly he gets up and
shuffles out of the office.*

Magistrates Court

BLACK:
A few days after this, David was in court
again.
March 1969:

CLERK:
There are two charges here of trespassing and two
of disorderly conduct.
Do you understand the charges?

Magistrates Court (later)

Thirty days.

BLACK:
Discharge: 10th April, 1969.

In Prison

We see DAVID *and* P.W.O. *in his
cell.*

BLACK:
Prison Welfare Officer's report:

P.W.O.:
Nowhere to go on release.
Rapidly becoming a social problem.
It is increasingly obvious that he is
completely unable to function on the
outside.
It was quite impossible to get through to
him.
He seemed schizoid to me,
one wonders whether or not
he was capable of knowing what
the discussion was all about.

P.W.O. *leaves*
DAVID *sits alone in his cell.*
Silence.

Mary's Office

DAVID *and* MARY *sit.*

MARY:
10th April, 1969.
The Nigerian was not excitable, but it was
almost impossible to understand him.
He said he had £1 19s., which was his own
money
and he would have no difficulty in finding
an address
if he could have a little more.
I gave him a letter to the M.O.S.S.,
and told him to go straight there.

Mary's Office (later)

We see MARY *phoning.*

MARY:
After he'd gone I phoned the manager
and explained the situation,
and he said they would do what they could
to help him,
so that he will have some money to put down
for lodgings.

Social Security Offices

DAVID *waits in a queue.*

WHITE:
David went to the Social Security and
picked up his money.

84

DAVID *is given money.*

BLACK:
He had eight days to live.

DAY OF THE DROWNING

A Street

Having left the offices of the Social Security,
DAVID *wanders round the streets.*

WHITE:
In this, the last week of his life,
David, sick, shuffled about the streets,
carrying the briefcase full of old
newspapers
that kept him warm during the night.

A Shop Doorway

DAVID *sleeps.*

Street (night)

WHITE:
He slept in shop doorways, under railway
arches.

Again we see DAVID *asleep.*

BLACK:
April 18th, 1969.
The alleged day of David's death.

The Bridal House

DAVID *lies sleeping.*

WHITE:
Three hours before David is thought to
have died.

The Sergeant again discovered him sleeping
in a doorway,
and called the Inspector.

> *We hear* COBB'S *voice describe this. The
> camera moves back so that we can see only the
> outside of the Bridal House.*

COBB:
The Inspector arrived armed with a
truncheon.
There was no question of the Nigerian being
violent.
So far as everyone knew, he was found
asleep.
The police officers went into the doorway.

> *We don't see what follows,*
> *but there are shouts and there is*
> *the noise of blows.*

CONSTABLE:
. . . I heard blows being struck . . .

> DAVID *runs from the Bridal*
> *House,*
> *covering his head with his arms.*
> *The* INSPECTOR *and the* SERGEANT
> *come out.*
> *They are smiling.*

COBB:
The Inspector told the policeman who was
watching
to make a false entry in his pocket book.
If the Nigerian were to complain,
the Inspector would then demonstrate
that he was several hundred yards away.

In Crown Court

COBB:
It is the case for the Crown that apart
from these two men,
no one who knew or was acquainted with the
Nigerian
ever saw him alive again
after he had run up Lands Lane shortly
after 3 a.m.

A Street

DAVID *is limping along.*
The TWO POLICEMEN *have given chase.*

Riverside

*There is the sound of single
running feet,
then* DAVID *runs towards us, trips,
and falls into the River Aire.
He screams as he falls.*

The River

*The River Aire at this point is about
thirty feet wide.
It runs between high stone-walled
banks and is about six feet deep.
Various shots show the swirling
waters carry away* DAVID'S *body.
The sound of the splash dies slowly
away.*

Townscape

*Various shots show the deserted
town.
It is five o'clock in the morning.*

We hear the voice of

BLACK:
Later, the Sergeant and the Inspector were found
guilty of three and four of the charges
of assault respectively. They went to
prison for two years and for three years.

We hear the voice of the

INSPECTOR'S WIFE:
I went to see my husband in gaol.
I came away feeling ill, the change in him
was so terrible.
He looked haggard and drawn,
but was so pleased to see us.
He is still the same husband and still the
same father.
He thought the police was the most wonderful job in the world
and he would have nothing said against
them.
The only thing I want to say to
people is
that if anyone criticizes they ought to
think,
'There but for the grace of God go I.'

Derelict Land

Some DOSSERS *asleep.*

WHITE:
If only we could find some better way than
prison.
Some better way that made men better . . .
not worse . . .

Meadow by a River

*Spring flowers are growing by a
river and* CHILDREN *are playing.*

A Graveyard

*The grave is on high ground.
There are tower blocks of flats
visible around, the big chimneys
of factories, housing estates, a
clock tower.
Beech trees arch overhead and round
the common graves a few makeshift
crosses have been set up.
Song; 'Jerusalem', continues to the
end of the film.
We see the tombstone with, at the
bottom of eight other names, the
name of* DAVID OLUWALE.

Street Corner

*At a windy, street corner we see,
scrawled on the wall, the words;
'REMEMBER OLUWALE'.*

The River

DAVID'S *face, c.u., smiles at us
from under water.
Credits over.*

THE END

THE SINGLE HOMELESS

Some thoughts on the death of
David Oluwale.

Who was responsible for the death of this man?

Was it the sadistic tendencies of two members of a city's Police Force?

Was it some will to death in David Oluwale?

Was it the high price placed on success back home in Nigeria which made it impossible for him to return?

Was it the Psychiatric Hospital which turned him out twice when many would say that he was incapable of surviving outside on his own?

Was it the Prison Welfare Department who, while expressing doubts as to his ability to survive outside, none the less did not, after '65 send him to the Psychiatric Hospital or otherwise intervene?

Was it the Mental Health Act (1959) which recommended that people like him who were not dangerously mad should not be in Psychiatric Hospital?

Was it the Supplementary Benefits Commission, who, since the war had steadily been closing down their hostels?

Was it the failure of Local Authorities to provide sufficient alternative accommodation as recommended in the Act?

Was it the various charities who claim to be providing accommodation for this part of the population?

Was it that curious custom of moving vagrants on?

Perhaps better say, despite many kind people in it, it was a malfunctioning of the Welfare State as a whole.

For our Welfare State was designed precisely so that people would not fall through the bottom of the net as David did.

It was designed so that there would be no more punishment of failure.

David Oluwale failed, and he was punished.

The death of this man took place in Leeds.

But the aim of this film is not to point an accusing finger at Leeds City in general or those two policemen in particular.

David's tragic death is an extreme example of something that is happening all over Britain: the harrassing of the unwanted.

Doctor Farrukh Hashmi has identified 'five stages of prejudice'; anti-locution; avoidance; discrimination; physical attack; extermination.

94

David passed through all stages.

Mr. Alec Muir, Chief Constable of Durham,
is reported as having 'calmly defended the
logic of his personal view, that criminals
should be quietly eliminated, rather than
locked away'.

A Midlands Councillor has also claimed on the
BBC that 'one must exterminate the
impossibles'.

'But exterminate is a terrible word,' said his
interviewer; 'Do you really mean that?'

And the Councillor said; 'Why not?'

David Oluwale

David lived in this house, 209, Belle Vue Road, Leeds, with Gladys.

A pub at Bramhope to which David was taken by car, told to ask for a cup of tea at 4.40 a.m., and abandoned.

Middleton Woods, to which David was taken by car at night and abandoned.

*The Bridal House, The Headrow, Leeds, in whose porch
David often used to sleep and was assaulted.*

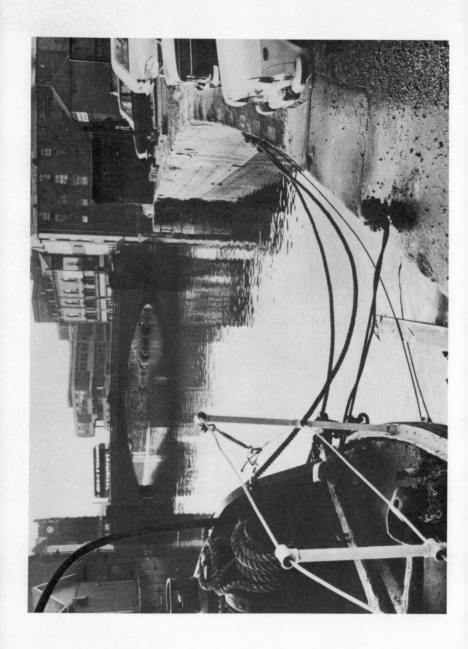

The River Aire at the point at which David died.
'... He is said to have entered the river from a point on the wharfside near the parked car on the right of the picture. His last meeting with the Sergeant and Inspector was further up the street near the bridge.'

GA 041002

CERTIFIED COPY OF AN ENTRY
Pursuant to the Births and **Deaths Registration Act 1953**

DEATH	Entry No. 96

Registration district	Leeds	Administrative area
Sub-district	Leeds	County Borough of Leeds

1. Date and place of death

Dead body found 4.5.69.- River Aire

2. Name and surname	3. Sex	Male
David OLUWALE otherwise known as ALLIWALA	4. Maiden surname of woman who has married	-----

5. Date and place of birth   30-8-30
Lagos

6. Occupation and usual address   Tailor
No fixed abode

7. (a) Name and surname of informant	(b) Qualification
Certificate received from D.Bywater Coroner	for Leeds Inquest held 14th May 1969

(c) Usual address   ------------------------------

8. Cause of death

FOUND DROWNED

9 I certify that the particulars given by me above are true to the best of my knowledge and belief

------------------------   Signature
.... of informant

10. Date of registration	11. Signature of registrar
Third June 1969	H.Grigg Registrar

David's death certificate.

David's tombstone.

Police later dug up David's body for an autopsy.

The graveyard.

THE RIGHT TO LIVE?

Has a man the right to kill himself in whatever way he chooses?

Has he the right to live how he chooses, provided he doesn't harm others? Has a man the right to live rough, has he the right to draw only those benefits that he wants from society?

Has he the right to eschew houses, regular meals, smart clothes, a job, all the trappings that make up our idea of how a respectable human *should* live? Who was David Oluwale offending by sleeping in shop doorways, or under railway bridges? Most towns in the world every night accept such people.

British towns do not, and the simplest answer, now come to be recognized by both Government and those engaged in social work, would appear to lie with the small permissive hostel, run by a kindly father figure who will make no rules, ask not too many questions, but who will supply a bed for the night.

Such a solution is far cheaper to the taxpayer than the expensive succession of prisons and psychiatric hospitals and courts that David went through; far more humane than the quite inappropriate treatment he received in every one of these places.

Many thousands of people sleep rough each night in Britain.

The man who sleeps rough on a cold December night is not there out of choice, surely?

They are there tonight and they will be there tomorrow night . . . the thousands of people who, when the rest of us are in our beds, are out there sleeping rough in shop doorways, derelict buildings, railway stations, deserted railway carriages, barns, air-raid shelters, beach huts, under the sky; wrapped in newspapers, old sacks, old clothes, straw.

And beyond these thousands there stretch other greater thousands—those who spend their lives in the senseless solitary trek between common lodging-house, 'spike' (reception centre designed especially for down and outs), psychiatric hospital, and often, prison.

Many of the settled population have little time or pity for these anonymous lone 'single homeless' people. But there are two things which should be said here: first, there but for the grace of God go all of us; I have been amazed in these nether regions of Britain, how many were of high estate. And, second, those who do not pity them should consider how much it costs us in taxes to send them on their trek through a host of inappropriate social services and institutions.

In defining exactly who are the single homeless, I think the question of intention is important. Jesus Christ was a propertyless vagrant and advocated this way of life but few would say that he was homeless in the sense that he was in need of help. Most people in prison or psychiatric hospital are there because society has decided that that is the best place for them to be.

The ones who are amongst the single homeless in the sense of being in need are those who are there, not because that is where they ought to be, but because nowhere more appropriate can be found to put them. There are thousands of people in these places who needed a roof over their heads and a relatively unpressurized set-up. What they actually get is expensive treatment designed to do something quite else; at great cost to the rest of us.

I think that the Supplementary Benefits Commission is most to blame in this. The National Assistance Act and later Acts require them to make 'provision whereby persons without a settled way of life might be influenced to lead a more settled life'.

Their quaint interpretation of this duty has been, since the Act, to reduce the number of 'spikes' from over three hundred to little more than twenty. And so charities struggle on, amidst impossible odds, to do their duty for them.

Local Authorities, though, have similar duties or powers. They have a duty to provide temporary accommodation for those 'whose homelessness could not reasonably have been foreseen or in such other circumstances as the authority may in any particular case determine' (National Assistance Act). They have powers to build subsidized hostels for ex-offenders (Criminal Justice Act).

'They should be put on a train.' A Midlands Councillor said this when he was on Television with me as his solution to the problem of down and outs sleeping rough in Wolverhampton. Hearing his words, I wondered where the train he had in mind was going to?

As standards become higher in Britain, so the number of people who cannot attain to these standards seems to grow greater. A disturbing metaphor compares the increasing flow of dropouts and down and outs to what emerges from the waste pipes taking unrecyclable material from an increasingly productive modern factory.

The human waste in the sump of society is people with their own sensitivity and dignity. They are threatened by other things as well as by standards to which they cannot aspire.

This is one of the most overcrowded countries in the world and many people now are beginning to feel the squash. Along with the dislike of other forms of pollution there seems to be growing up a dislike of what some people think of as 'human pollution'. One of the explanations given for the harassing by police of David is that Leeds City police were proud of their city and 'liked to have a clean city'.

Another reason for the increase in the number of dropouts may be that those glossy stereotypes of what we should be flashed so constantly at us by the Telly make it harder to accept those people who conform less rather than more to these stereotypes; makes many people now want to sweep under the carpet those who are not 'normal'; makes them feel that the Welfare State has no need to stretch itself as far as those whose abnormal behaviour makes it quite clear that they're *not trying*: the epileptics, hippies, elderly, Bohemians, beats, mentally subnormal . . .

Whatever the reason, many State institutions and many charities evaded their responsibilities, whether given them by Parliament or self-assumed, where David was concerned.

Many of those turned loose from psychiatric hospital after the '59 Act ended up in the various spikes just as David did, and there has been quite an interesting official silence on this point.

The biggest State spike still in existence is at Camberwell and this sleeps about 700 a night and through its doors about 3,000 people pass a year.

Of these, reliable estimates say that about a third have been in psychiatric hospital.

As early as 1966 the London Consultative Committee for the single homeless wrote to the Department of Health about the way that people removed from psychiatric hospital ended up in a dosshouse.

This letter was ignored. Later another letter was written.

More recently a report was submitted in long form early in 1972 and in August '73 in a shorter version. This also was ignored.

One way of looking at what has happened in our psychiatric hospitals is by seeing them as successors to the old poorhouses. The poorhouse was meant to cope with everyone but in fact they couldn't cope with their mad people so they farmed them out to private madhouses which resulted in various scandals in the early nineteenth century.

And then the psychiatric hospitals began to be built. This went on for some time until, with the '59 Act, came the emptying of the hospitals. One reason for their emptying was that these places no longer deemed it as part of their function to provide 'care and protection' for their inmates, as well as treatment. The old Poor Law idea of 'care and protection' had been lost.

The old idea of 'care and protection' has also been lost in medical hospitals. These places now won't take people that they think they can do nothing for, and sometimes indeed write 'not to be readmitted' on such people's cards.

The psychiatrist David Tidmarsh has been working on studies of the history of various other dossers who exemplify, in the way that Oluwale did, our failure to succour those in need at the bottom of our society.

One former psychiatric patient of his, for instance, was found not so long ago beaten unconscious in London, and, at the time of writing, had not returned to consciousness.

Tidmarsh suggests that the following provisions should have been incorporated in the 1959 Act;

Adequate financial backing should have been given to Local Authorities for them to build hostels and other facilities for community care.

The provision of such places should have been made mandatory.

There should have been provision for investigation to have taken place after the event to see whether it had worked.

How many new recruits are there to that shadowy world inhabited by David Oluwale.

At the end of 1972, in the course of the 'Crisis at Christmas' campaign, it was claimed that there had been 'incredible increases' in the number of homeless teenagers, with at least 8,000 in the Central London area alone sleeping rough each night.

The problem, it was said, is a growing one and the statutory services are ignoring their plight.

Jon Snow, co-ordinator of the New Horizon centre in London, said that the last two years had shown dramatic increases in the number of kids adrift in Central London.

'They are fifteen, sixteen, seventeen and eighteen year olds going to seed in the centre of an ugly hostile city in which statutory social services deny all responsibility.'

This figure, he said, does not count tourists. 'The homeless youngsters sleep in parks, derelict buildings, under bridges and in seedy all-night cafés and clubs. 'Very little is known and even less is said about young homeless people and yet this is a section of the community in which homelessness has developed most dramatically within the last five years.

'Homeless young people are written off as hippy dropouts in search of some alternative way of life. The truth is very far removed from that, if our experience at New Horizon is anything to go by.'

He said that over 2,000 individuals had come through his day centre so far this year. He estimated that 80 per cent came from the provinces and 50 per cent from greater Glasgow.

Thirty per cent of them came from some sort of child care situation. Others came from collapsed families, Approved School, Borstal, and prison. All were united in that they were homeless and rootless.

A typical case was a girl called Sue, aged fifteen, who left Dundee for London to escape a broken home situation. She had already been in care several times. She had three pounds when she arrived and spent that on her first night on bed and breakfast.

The next day she sought work without success and the next night went to the police. They sent her to the emergency Social Security office. They were unable to provide her with accommodation at their hostel at Great Guildford Street. Finally she was given 50p and told to come back in the morning.

She drifted into the West End to an amusement arcade and there met a group of homeless teenagers who had been living in a derelict house in Covent Garden.

Jon Snow commented; 'When we came across her she was by now pregnant; with a child well on the way to going into care like its mother.

'Sue to some extent is typical. She made no conscious attempt to drop or opt out of life . . . she was never really in a position to choose. She was a disorientated and lonely individual who had landed in the West End at the end of a chain of circumstances over which she herself had little or no control.'

Later at the same meeting the Rev. James A. E. Martin. M.B.E. said that 'all agencies, voluntary bodies and reception centres are experiencing an increase in the number of homeless seeking help'.

Since then, there has been no reverse in this trend. Large dosshouses have closed, bureaucrats continue to pass the buck. However, some small organizations have been able to extend their network of small, charitable hostels. If David Oluwale had happened on one of these, he need not have died.

SELECT BIBLIOGRAPHY

Holloway, J. *They Can't Fit In: A Study of Destitute Men Under 30, in St. Georges Crypt, Leeds.* London National Council of Social Service, 1970.

Lebon, Charlotte. *A Cyrenian Handbook.* The Cyrenians Ltd., 7, Sole Street, Crundale, Canterbury.

O'Connor, Philip. *Britain in the Sixties; Vagrancy.* Penguin, 1963.

Parker, Tony, *The Unknown Citizen.* Hutchinson, 1963, Penguin, 1967.

Parker, Tony. *People of the Streets.* Jonathan Cape, 1968.

Breed, Brian. *The Man Outside.* Epworth Press, 1967.

Sandford, Jeremy. *Edna, the Inebriate Woman.* London, Pan, 1971.

Sandford, Jeremy. *Down and Out in Britain.* N.E.L. 1972.

Toomey, Lee. *Down and Out.* Wayland, 1973.

Trench, S. *Bury Me in My Boots.* Hodder and Stoughton, 1968.

Turner, Merfyn. *Forgotten Men.* National Council of Social Service, 26, Bedford Square, London, W.C.1. 1960.

The NACRO Directory. (NACRO is the National Association for the Care and Resettlement of the Offender), 125, Kennington Park Road, London, S.E.11.

Mathews, Gordon and Creed, Angela (Eds.) *Where to House the Single Homeless – who decides?* The Cyrenians, 13, Windcheap, Canterbury, Kent, 1974.

Homeless Single People in Need of Care and Support. DHSS. 1972.